TABLE OF CONTENTS

For the Teacher

This reproducible study guide to use in conjunction with the novel *The Outsiders* consists of lessons for guided reading. Written in chapter-by-chapter format, the guide contains a synopsis, pre-reading activities, vocabulary and comprehension exercises, as well as extension activities to be used as follow-up to the novel.

In a homogeneous classroom, whole class instruction with one title is appropriate. In a heterogeneous classroom, reading groups should be formed: each group works on a different novel at its own reading level. Depending upon the length of time devoted to reading in the classroom, each novel, with its guide and accompanying lessons, may be completed in three to six weeks.

Begin using NOVEL-TIES for reading development by distributing the novel and a folder to each student. Distribute duplicated pages of the study guide for students to place in their folders. After examining the cover and glancing through the book, students can participate in several pre-reading activities. Vocabulary questions should be considered prior to reading a chapter; all other work should be done after the chapter has been read. Comprehension questions can be answered orally or in writing. The classroom teacher should determine the amount of work to be assigned, always keeping in mind that readers must be nurtured and that the ultimate goal is encouraging students' love of reading.

The benefits of using NOVEL-TIES are numerous. Students read good literature in the original, rather than in abridged or edited form. The good reading habits, formed by practice in focusing on interpretive comprehension and literary techniques, will be transferred to the books students read independently. Passive readers become active, avid readers.

SYNOPSIS

Ponyboy Curtis and his two older brothers, Darry and Sodapop, come from the "wrong side of town." Since the death of their parents, Darry has been trying to keep the family together. Their only real sense of belonging comes from their fellow gang members, the Greasers. The Greasers, with their long hair, tight tee-shirts, and leather jackets are constantly at war with the Socs, a gang of affluent boys who dress in madras jackets and smell of English Leather cologne. Both Ponyboy and his friend Johnny have been attacked by Socs, who left them bruised and beaten.

One evening, Bob and his fellow Socs gang members see Ponyboy and Johnny walking with Cherry and her friend Marcia. Angered that these Greasers are with Socs' girls, Bob and his friends attack them. When Bob puts Ponyboy's head under the fountain, Johnny retaliates by pulling a switchblade, fatally wounding Bob. Dally, a fellow Greaser, gives the boys money and a gun, advising them to hide in an abandoned church in another town.

Alone and frightened at the hideout, the boys smoke cigarettes while Ponyboy reads *Gone With the Wind* to Johnny. After Dally visits, bringing news from home, Johnny and Ponyboy decide to return and face the consequences of the night in the park. Before they can carry out their plan, they learn that the neighborhood church is on fire. In an attempt to save some local children caught in the fire, the boys are burned and injured.

Although Johnny and Ponyboy are lauded as heroes, their fortunes do not improve. Johnny does not survive his injuries; Dally is killed by police after robbing a grocery store; and the court must determine whether Ponyboy will remain under his brother's care. Grateful that the judge allows the brothers to stay together, Ponyboy must now try to put his life back together. He is inspired by a message left in their copy of *Gone With the Wind* in which Johnny wrote that there is good and beauty in life and that Ponyboy can become whatever he wants to be.

PRE-READING ACTIVITIES

1. Preview the book by reading the title and the author's name and by looking at the illustration on the cover. What do you think the book will be about? Where and when does the story take place? Have you read any other books by the same author?

2. A "peer" is someone who is equal to another in age, background, and social status. Who are your peers? Do you ever feel pressure to dress or to act like your peers? Have you ever done anything you didn't want to do because of peer pressure? Do you think young children, teenagers, or adults are more affected by peer pressure?

3. **Cooperative Learning Activity:** Work with a small group of your classmates to discuss times when bad behavior was caused by peer pressure. Compile a list of strategies that may be used to resist peer pressure. Compare your responses to those of other groups in your class.

4. Are there any gangs in your school or your neighborhood? Why do you think gangs form? Who joins gangs? Do you think gangs are more likely to form in cities, suburbs, or rural areas? Do you think gangs should be allowed to operate, or should they be banned?

5. Find newspaper articles reporting on gang activity. Where do gangs exist? Are they responsible for any violent activity? Are there any efforts to curb their activity?

6. What different social groups exist in your school? Do they get along? Is there a good social climate in your school? Do you have any suggestions for improving the social climate?

7. Slang, a vocabulary peculiar to a particular group, class, or profession, can make a story seem authentic. Here is a list of some of the slang expressions found in this novel. What does each one mean? Which ones seem old-fashioned? Do you know any current expressions which are similar to any of these?
    *   greaser
    *   to dig something
    *   to bug someone
    *   blade
    *   heater
    *   rumble
    *   half-crocked
    *   to know the score
    *   a chip off the old block
    *   weed
    *   play chicken
    *   fuzz
    *   boozehound

CHAPTER 1

Vocabulary: Each boldfaced word is shown with a standard and a slang definition. Look at each pair of sentences, choose the meaning that fits the way the underlined word is used and write the letter of the correct definition on the line to the right. Then write "S" next to the slang definition.

hot
    a. having a high temperature
    b. recently stolen

1. On a <u>hot</u>, sweltering day, we like to go to the beach to cool off. _____

2. He was arrested for dealing in <u>hot</u> jewelry. _____

blast
    a. event that is a lot of fun
    b. gust of wind

3. A <u>blast</u> of cold air sent shivers up my spine. _____

4. That party was a <u>blast</u>. _____

drag
    a. dull or boring situation or person
    b. pull along the ground

5. Doing all that homework can be a real <u>drag</u>. _____

6. Please don't <u>drag</u> that jacket on the floor. _____

lift
    a. steal
    b. raise; bring to a higher place

7. The gang tried to <u>lift</u> the hubcaps before the police came. _____

8. <u>Lift</u> that box onto the truck. _____

rumble
a. deep, heavy sound
b. fight

9. The flash of lightning and the <u>rumble</u> of thunder scared him. _____

10. Ponyboy did not want to join in the <u>rumble</u>. _____

Chapter 1 (cont.)

> Read to learn who are the Socs and the Greasers.

Questions:

1. How were the Socs and the Greasers alike? How were they different?

2. What happened to Ponyboy on the way home from the movies? Why did this happen?

3. How did the other Greasers react when they found Ponyboy?

4. According to Sodapop, why did Darry get upset with Ponyboy?

5. How were Ponyboy and his brothers different from other hoods or greasers?

Questions for Discussion:

1. Why do you think some boys became Greasers? Why did some become Socs?

2. In what ways were the boys' lives better and worse for becoming gang members?

Literary Devices:

I. *Simile*—A simile is a figure of speech in which two unlike objects are compared using the words "like" or "as." For example:

> Soda attracted girls like honey draws flies.

What is being compared?

_____

Why is this better than just saying that Soda attracted girls?

_____

II. *Point of View*—The point of view in fiction refers to the person telling the story. A story told in the first person is narrated by a character in the story. A story told in the third person is narrated by the author.

From whose point of view is this story told?

_____

Why do you think the author chose this point of view?

_____

_____

Chapter 1 (cont.)

Literary Element: Characterization

The opening chapter of this book introduces the reader to many of the important characters. Fill in the following chart based upon information found in this chapter. Add to this chart as you continue to read.

	Physical Description	**Personality Traits**
Ponyboy		
Sodapop		
Darry		
Steve Randle		
Two-Bit Matthews		
Dally Winston		
Johnny Cade		

Writing Activity:

Reread the author's descriptions of each important character introduced in Chapter One. In a short paragraph tell which character you might want to have as a friend and why this person would be a good friend.

CHAPTER 2

Vocabulary: Analogies are equations in which the first pair of words has the same relationship as the second pair of words. For example: DAY is to NIGHT as GOODNESS is to EVIL. Both pairs of words are opposites. Choose the best word from the Word Box to complete each of the analogies below.

```
                        WORD BOX
    bicker      law-abiding      roguish
    fiery       nonchalant       scatterbrained
```

1. HAPPY is to CHEERFUL as CASUAL is to _____.

2. GENTLE is to ROUGH as CALM is to _____.

3. DECENT is to GENTLEMAN as _____ is to SCOUNDREL.

4. HONEST is to _____ as DISHONEST is to CRIMINAL.

5. SENSIBLE is to WISE as _____ is to FOOLISH.

6. FRIEND is to ENEMY as AGREE is to _____.

> Read to find out why the Greasers and the Socs were enemies.

Questions:

1. How did Ponyboy and the Greasers spend their time?

2. Why did Dally break laws?

3. Why was it surprising that Cherry was attracted to Dally?

4. Describe the rules of a "fair" gang fight.

5. Why do you think Ponyboy and the other Greasers resented the Socs?

Question for Discussion:

Do you think a gang fight is legitimate if it follows the rules of a "fair" fight?

Chapter 2 (cont.)

Literary Device: Flashback

A flashback is a device in which an author interrupts a story in order to relate an event that happened at an earlier time.

What past event did the author relate?

_____

_____

Why did the author use a flashback in this chapter?

_____

_____

Why was the information in the flashback important?

_____

_____

Writing Activity:

Imagine that you are Cherry. Write a journal entry describing your evening with Ponyboy and Johnny.

CHAPTER 3

Vocabulary: Synonyms are words with similar meanings. Circle the letter of the synonym for the underlined word in each of the following sentences.

1. The man <u>gallantly</u> carried the child out of the burning building to safety.

   a. bravely   b. angrily   c. quickly   d. tragically

2. Because of his shyness, the young man had the reputation of being <u>aloof</u>.

   a. curiosity   b. pleasure   c. standoffish   d. inquisitive

3. The <u>ornery</u> child threw his cereal on the floor in a tantrum.

   a. lonely   b. silly   c. placid   d. mean-tempered

4. The <u>cunning</u> thief tricked the residents into letting him into their house.

   a. sly   b. beautiful   c. shy   d. fortunate

5. Once cornered, the bank robbers <u>resignedly</u> went with the police officers.

   a. unhappily   b. unresistingly   c. slowly   d. happily

> Read to find out if Ponyboy runs away.

Questions:

1. According to Cherry, how were the Greasers and the Socs different? What made Ponyboy feel that they were not completely different?

2. How had life been unfair to the Greasers?

3. What did Ponyboy mean when he said as he awoke in the field "the stars have moved"?

4. How did Darry react when Ponyboy finally came home? Why did he act this way?

5. What did Ponyboy decide to do to change his life? Why did he change his mind?

Questions for Discussion:

1. Cherry told Ponyboy that the Socs wanted to be "cool to the point of not feeling anything." Do you and your friends try to be "cool? Do you think it is possible to be too cool?

2. Why do you think Ponyboy was happy to realize that both he and Cherry saw the same sunsets?

Chapter 3 (cont.)

Literary Device: Cliffhanger

A cliffhanger in literature is a device borrowed from silent serialized films in which an episode ended at a moment of high tension or suspense. In a book it is usually placed at the end of a chapter to encourage the reader to continue on to the next part. What is the cliffhanger at the end of Chapter Three?

_____

_____

Graphics Organizer:

Use the Venn diagram below to compare the Greasers and the Socs. Record the ways they are alike in the overlapping part of the circles.

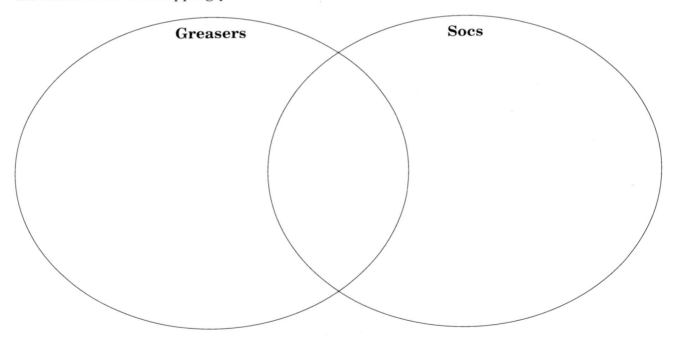

Writing Activity:

Write about someone you know in whom you can confide as openly as Ponyboy does with Cherry. Without revealing confidences that you have shared, describe this person and explain why you are able to tell this person your secrets.

CHAPTER 4

Vocabulary: Draw a line from each word on the left to its meaning on the right. Then use the numbered words to fill in the blanks in the paragraph below.

1.	territory	a.	dazed from exhaustion or blows
2.	unceasingly	b.	keeping oneself from harm or injury
3	bootlegging	c.	tract of land; district
4.	apprehension	d.	endlessly
5.	self-preservation	e.	showing a hateful, disrespectful expression
6.	contemptuously	f.	selling something illegally
7.	groggy	g.	uneasiness; fear
8.	reformatory	h.	penal institution to reform young offenders

. . . .

Peter had never been in trouble before. Now he was on his way to the state

_____^{1} on charges of _____.^{2} Peter felt _____^{3} because

he had not slept. The train rattled _____^{4} during the entire trip. As they came

nearer to the institution, the boy became filled with _____.^{5} The prison would

be unfamiliar _____^{6} to Peter. He was afraid the other prisoners would treat

him _____^{7} because he was so young. "I must learn the art of _____^{8}

here, thought Peter, "if I'm going to make it."

> Read to find out why Ponyboy and Johnny went into hiding.

Questions:

1. Why did the Socs come looking for Ponyboy and Johnny?
2. Why did Johnny behave in an uncharacteristically violent way?
3. Why did Ponyboy and Johnny turn to Dally for help? What did he do for them?
4. Why did Ponyboy feel that he and Johnny would be in hiding for the rest of their lives?

Chapter 4 (cont.)

Questions for Discussion:

1. Do you think Ponyboy and Johnny had to run away? What other choices could they have made?

2. What do you think Darry and Sodapop will do when they discover Ponyboy is missing? What might be happening in the Curtis household?

Writing Activity:

This exciting point in the novel could be dramatized. Set the scene in the abandoned church. Write dialogue that could be spoken by Ponyboy and Johnny. They can review the events that have brought them here and discuss their alternatives for future action. You may perform your scene with a classmate.

CHAPTER 5

Vocabulary: Antonyms are words with opposite meanings. Draw a line from each word in column A to its antonym in column B. Then use the words in column A to fill in the blanks in the sentences below.

	A		B
1.	reluctantly	a.	unhealthy
2.	eluded	b.	demanding
3.	sullen	c.	eagerly
4.	vital	d.	attracted
5.	imploring	e.	joyous

. . . .

1. We couldn't resist the little boy's _____ glance as he noticed the cookies on the plate.

2. No matter how hard I studied advanced algebra, the correct answers to problems always _____ me.

3. I _____ allowed the girls to travel alone to the city.

4. In order to have a(n) _____ green plant, you must water it and let it have some sunshine each day.

5. Her _____ expression and bad temper made it hard for her to gain new friends.

> Read to find out how Ponyboy and Johnny spend their time in hiding.

Questions:

1. How did Ponyboy feel when he awoke in the church?

2. What evidence showed that Johnny did care for Ponyboy?

3. Why did the boys change their hair style? Why was this hard for them to do?

4. How did the boys pass the time in the church?

5. How did Johnny feel about Dally? Why did he feel this way?

6. What information did Dally bring to the boys?

Chapter 5 (cont.)

Questions for Discussion:

1. *Gone With the Wind* is a romantic story about the South during the Civil War. Why do you think Johnny enjoyed reading it?

2. Reread Robert Frost's poem in this chapter. What do you think Frost is describing? Why did Ponyboy remember the poem?

Idioms:

Idioms are expressions that do not mean exactly what they say. Tell the meaning of the idioms below.

1. Johnny let me look in the old cracked mirror . . . I did a double take.

   _____

2. We killed time by playing poker.

   _____

3. I was dying for a cold drink on a hot day.

   _____

4. You look like you've been through the mill.

   _____

5. We both got a little green around the gills when Dally took a corner on two wheels with the brakes screaming.

   _____

Writing Activity:

Imagine that you have to go into hiding. Determine what ten things you would want to have with you. Then describe how you might spend a complete day while you are in the hideout.

CHAPTER 6

Vocabulary: Select the best synonym for the underlined word in each of the following sentences. Circle the letter of the word you choose.

1. He <u>doggedly</u> continued to look for his ring in the sand even after everyone else had gone home.

   a. tiredly   b. persistently   c. blindly   d. carelessly

2. Even though their water was running out, the victims had a strong <u>conviction</u> that they would be saved.

   a. belief   b. message   c. promise   d. trial

3. He <u>detached</u> the coupon from the newspaper before he brought it to the supermarket.

   a. opened   b. drove   c. carried   d. separated

4. Dad found a good piece of <u>timber</u> to replace the broken beam in the ceiling.

   a. insulation   b. concrete   c. wood   d. fabric

5. They gave him <u>plasma</u> after the accident.

   a. medicine   b. blood   c. food   d. bandages

> Read to find out what happens when the church goes on fire.

Questions:

1. Why did Cherry decide to help the Greasers?
2. Why did Johnny decide to turn himself in?
3. Why did Ponyboy and Johnny go into the burning church?
4. What happened to Johnny, Ponyboy, and Dally because of the fire?
5. When did Ponyboy realize that Darry really loved him?
6. How did Ponyboy feel about his life now that he understood Darry?

Questions for Discussion:

Do you think Ponyboy and Johnny acted heroically? Should they have left the safety of their hiding place? Would you have acted in a similar way?

Writing Activity:

An event like the fire in the church would be reported by local newspapers and television stations. Imagine you are a reporter covering this story and write an article for your newspaper. Be sure to include the important *who, what, why, when,* and *where* of the incident.

CHAPTER 7

Vocabulary: Draw a line from each word on the left to its definition on the right. Then use the numbered words to fill in the blanks in the sentences below.

1. mimic
2. palomino
3. manslaughter
4. genuine
5. recurring
6. aghast
7. individual

a. shocked; amazed
b. real
c. single; one
d. happening again and again
e. horse with a golden mane and tail
f. imitate
g. killing of a human being

. . . .

1. We gazed admiringly at the _____ in the pasture.

2. It is rude to _____ someone's behavior.

3. We put the gifts into _____ boxes so that each person would have a present to unwrap.

4. The audience was _____ when the aerialist fell off the tightrope.

5. _____ is a serious crime demanding a harsh penalty.

6. I became afraid to go to sleep at night because of a(n) _____ nightmare.

7. It is hard to tell a(n) _____ pearl from a good fake.

> Read to find out how the fire changed the boys' lives.

Questions:

1. Why were television reporters interested in what happened to Ponyboy and Johnny?

2. What was Johnny's physical condition after the fire? How did Ponyboy think this would affect Johnny's life?

3. What information did Ponyboy learn from the newspaper?

4. Why did Randy want to talk to Ponyboy?

5. Why didn't Randy want to fight in the upcoming rumble?

6. What important discovery about individuals did Randy and Ponyboy make when they met at Tasty Freeze?

Chapter 7 (cont.)

Questions for Discussion:

Why do you think people sometimes act in an uncharacteristic way when they are in a group or a gang? Has this ever happened to you?

Writing Activity:

Imagine you are a judge who must decide the fate of Ponyboy and Sodapop. What decision would you reach? In a brief paragraph tell where you think the two boys should live and how you came to your conclusion.

CHAPTER 8

Vocabulary: Draw a line from each word on the left to its meaning on the right. Then use the numbered words to fill in the blanks in the sentences below.

1. numb
2. faltered
3. quivering
4. resemblance
5. debate
6. charitable

a. likeness in appearance
b. generous
c. lacking emotion or feeling
d. hesitated in action or purpose
e. shaking with a slight, rapid motion
f. consider both sides of an argument

. . . .

1. The runner _____ as he neared the finish line, which caused him to lose the race by a second.

2. The twins had such a striking _____ to one another that people were constantly getting them confused.

3. She was such a _____ woman that a building at the university was named after her.

4. The political candidates will _____ the issue of gun control before the election.

5. We observed his lips _____ with emotion as he tried to hold back tears.

6. The flood victims stood quietly beside their destroyed homes, apparently _____ from the shock.

> Read to find out about Ponyboy's and Johnny's hospital experience.

Questions:

1. Why did the doctor allow the boys to see Johnny?

2. What did Ponyboy mean when he considered, "Sixteen years on the streets and you see a lot. But all the wrong sights, not the sights you want to see"?

3. Why did Johnny refuse to see his mother?

4. What was Dally going to do with Two-Bit's knife?

5. Why was Ponyboy upset with Cherry?

Chapter 8 (cont.)

Questions for Discussion:

1. Do you think there could be any way to stop the fight between the Greasers and the Socs?

2. What might a social worker or a counselor do to maintain peace between the two gangs?

Writing Activity:

Write about a time when you or someone you know had to face a dangerous situation. Describe the situation, tell why it could not be avoided, and then tell what finally happened.

CHAPTER 9

Vocabulary: Use the context to figure out the meaning of the underlined word in each of the following sentences. In the chart below, write what you think the word means. Then compare your definition with a dictionary definition.

- The baby looks like a <u>miniature</u> version of his father.
- The child <u>grimaced</u> as the doctor gave her an injection.
- He looked at me with <u>mock</u> horror when I told him the plant had died.
- Mr. Smith used an <u>amplifier</u> to broadcast his speech to the neighborhood.
- Amy went to the dance alone because she didn't have an <u>escort</u>.

	Your Definition	**Dictionary Definition**
1. miniature		
2. grimaced		
3. mock		
4. amplifier		
5. escort		

> Read to find out how the Greasers got ready for the fight.

Questions:

1. What preparations did Ponyboy make before the fight? Why did he do this?

2. Why was Darry concerned about Ponyboy's involvement in the fight?

3. Why did Dally want Ponyboy to be tough and hard like him rather than be like Johnny? Do you think Dally believed his own advice?

4. What did Johnny mean when he told Ponyboy to "stay gold"?

Chapter 9 (cont.)

Questions for Discussion:

1. Do you think Ponyboy should listen to Dally's or Johnny's advice?

2. Do you think there is any good reason for fighting?

3. Why do you think Darry wants to fight Paul?

Literary Element: Characterization

Fighting appealed to each character for a different reason. Tell why each character was anxious to join the rumble.

Sodapop _____

_____

Darry _____

_____

Steve _____

_____

Two-Bit _____

_____

Dally _____

_____

Writing Activity:

Ponyboy came to understand that the Socs and the Greasers were equally tough, but most people judged the Greasers to be mean because of their appearances. Write about a time when you were fooled by appearances. Describe the contrast between appearance and reality in people or in an incident.

CHAPTER 10

Vocabulary: Use the words in the Word Box and the clues below to complete the crossword puzzle.

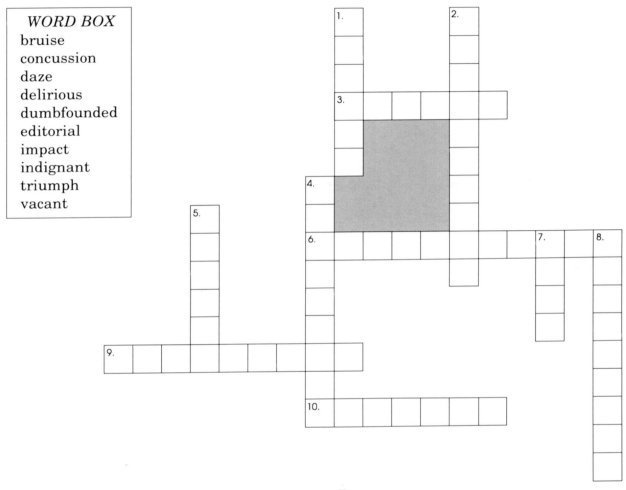

> *WORD BOX*
> bruise
> concussion
> daze
> delirious
> dumbfounded
> editorial
> impact
> indignant
> triumph
> vacant

Across

3. force of a strike to a body or object
6. made speechless with amazement
9. article presenting the opinion of the writer
10. satisfying victory or success

Down

1. injure without breaking the skin
2. violent shock or blow to the brain
4. feeling displeasure at something unjust
5. empty
7. state of confusion
8. in a condition of extreme restlessness in which hallucinations and uncontrolled speech are common

Read to find out how the fight ended.

Chapter 10 (cont.)

Questions:

1. Why did Ponyboy keep repeating that Johnny wasn't dead?

2. What happened to Dally? Do you think he planned what happened to him?

3. Why did Ponyboy believe that other Greasers would end up like Dally?

4. Why did Ponyboy end up in the hospital?

5. What did Ponyboy think about when he regained consciousness?

Question for Discussion:

How have Ponyboy's ideas about life changed since the beginning of the story and since the start of the rumble?

Writing Activity:

Imagine you are a reporter for a newspaper. Write an article describing what happened on the night of the rumble. Be sure to include the important facts about *who, what, when, where,* and *why* of the incident and its aftermath.

CHAPTERS 11, 12

Vocabulary: Draw a line from each word in column A to is antonym in column B. Then use the words in column A to fill in the blanks in the sentences below.

	A		B
1.	cautious	a.	limited
2.	calm	b.	wild
3.	familiar	c.	acquitted
4.	convicted	d.	clear
5.	vague	e.	reckless
6.	vast	f.	unknown

. . . .

1. I felt comfortable driving because I was on a _____ road.

2. In an emergency, it is important to stay _____ .

3. The instructions you gave me were so _____ that I got lost on the way to your house.

4. When traffic is heavy, it is good to obey the lights and be _____ as you cross the street.

5. We knew it would take many days to cross the _____ desert that lay before us.

6. You are more likely to be _____ of a crime if you have a criminal record.

> Read to find out what the judge decided.

Questions:

1. What did Ponyboy realize when he looked at Bob's picture?

2. Why did Randy visit Ponyboy?

3. Why was Ponyboy worried about the judge's decision at the hearing?

4. Why did Ponyboy keep saying that he killed Bob?

5. Why did the judge's questions surprise Ponyboy?

Chapters 11, 12 (cont.)

6. What decision did the judge make? What did this reveal about his character?

7. Why did Darry scold Ponyboy? Why did Sodapop become upset?

8. What message did Johnny send Ponyboy in the book? What do you think this letter revealed about Johnny?

9. What was Ponyboy's English theme? Why did he choose to write this?

Questions for Discussion:

1. Do you agree with Ponyboy that it is better to have others feel hatred toward you rather than pity?

2. Why do you think Darry called Ponyboy "little buddy" for the first time?

3. What messages do you think this book communicates?

Writing Activity:

If Socs and Greasers could sit down and talk so that each side could understand the other's feelings, what do you think they might tell each other? Construct an imaginary dialogue between some of the Greasers and some of the Socs.

CLOZE ACTIVITY

This excerpt is taken from Chapter Twelve. Read it through completely and then fill in the blanks with words that make sense. Then you may compare your language with that of the author.

Tell Dally. It was too _____ [1] to tell Dally. Would he have listened?

_____ [2] doubted it. Suddenly it wasn't only a _____ [3] thing to me.

I could picture hundreds _____ [4] hundreds of boys living on the wrong

_____ [5] of cities, boys with black eyes who _____ [6] at their own

shadows. Hundreds of boys who _____ [7] watched sunsets and looked at stars

and _____ [8] for something better. I could see boys _____ [9] down

under street lights because they were _____ [10] and tough and hated the world,

and _____ [11] was too late to tell them that _____ [12] was still good in

it, and they _____ [13] believe you if you did. It was _____ [14] vast a

problem to be just a _____ [15] thing. There should be some help, someone

_____ [16] tell them before it was too late. _____ [17] should tell their

side of the story, _____ [18] maybe people would understand then and wouldn't

_____ [19] so quick to judge a boy by _____ [20] amount of hair oil he

wore. It _____ [21] important to me. I picked up the _____ [22] book and

called my English teacher.

"Mr. Syme, this is Ponyboy. That theme—how long can it be?"

POST-READING ACTIVITIES

1. Return to the character chart that you began on page five of this study guide. Record additional information and then compare your responses with others who have read the same book.

2. Imagine that Ponyboy's parents had been alive. In what ways do you think this story would have been different?

3. What role do you think parents play in determining how their teenagers act outside the home? What role do you think their friends and classmates play in the way they behave?

4. Ponyboy came to realize that both rich and poor teenagers could have similar problems. What are some of the problems that all teenagers face?

5. Do you think that poverty or coming from a poor community is a reason to form gangs? Are there any positive things that could result from joining a gang?

6. To what extent did alcohol and drugs affect the behavior of the teenagers in this story? If this story were written today, do you think the influence of drugs and alcohol would be greater or less?

7. Check the newspapers for articles on gang fights, juvenile delinquency, violent teenage deaths, and other related topics. Determine whether the articles present a balanced picture or whether the information is slanted in any way. Compare these real life situations to the fictionalized experiences in the novel.

8. Write a letter to your local branch of Alcoholics Anonymous to find information on the teenage alcohol and drug problem in your locality.

9. With the help of your guidance counselor and school social worker, discuss community programs available to help young people find greater direction, purpose, and meaning in their lives. Are there a sufficient number of programs to meet the needs of teenagers?

10. Do some research to learn about the author S. E. Hinton. When was this book written? Why was it written? In what ways did the author make the story appealing to teenagers? Why do you think it has been popular for so many years?

11. Write a paragraph about each of the following main characters, briefly describing what you think each might be doing ten years after the time of the story:

Ponyboy	Darry	Sodapop	Two-Bit
Randy	Cherry	Steve	Tim

Post-Reading Activities (cont.)

12. **Fluency/Readers Theater:** Read a chapter of the book as though it were a play. Choose a chapter that has a lot of dialogue and has two or more characters in conversation. Select a classmate to read each role and then select another to read the narration. The characters should read only those words inside the quotation marks. Ignore phrases such as "he said" or "she said." You may want to use simple props, such as hats, to identify the characters, or small objects to identify the setting.

13. **Literature Circle:** Have a literature circle discussion in which you tell your personal reactions to *The Outsiders*. Here are some questions and sentence starters to help your literature circle begin a discussion.
    - How are you like any one of the characters in the novel? How are you different?
    - Did you find the characters in the novel realistic? Why or why not?
    - Which character did you like the most? The least?
    - Who else would you like to read this novel? Why?
    - What questions would you like to ask the author about the novel?
    - It was not fair when . . .
    - I would have liked to see . . .
    - I wonder . . .
    - Ponyboy learned that . . .

SUGGESTIONS FOR FURTHER READING

Beals, Melba Pattillo. *Warriors Don't Cry*. Simon Pulse.

Bonham, Frank. *Durango Street*. Puffin.

* Cormier, Robert. *The Chocolate War*. Laurel Leaf.

* _____. *Beyond the Chocolate War*. Laurel Leaf.

* Holman, Felice. *Slake's Limbo*. Aladdin.

Levoy, Myron. *A Shadow Like a Leopard*. Backinprint.com.

Lipsyte, Robert. *The Brave*. HarperCollins.

_____. *The Contender*. HarperCollins.

Lupica, Mike. *Fast Break*. Philomel Books.

Murphy, Jim. *Death Run*. Ticknor and Fields.

Myers, Walter Dean. *Hoops*. Ember.

_____. *Monster*. HarperCollins.

Sachar, Louis. *Holes*. Yearling.

* Spinelli, Jerry. *Maniac Magee*. Little Brown.

_____. *Wringer*. HarperCollins.

* Strasser, Todd. *The Wave*. Laurel Leaf.

* Swarthout, Glenn. *Bless the Beasts and Children*. Simon & Schuster.

Zindel, Paul. *I Never Loved Your Mind*. Starfire.

* _____. *The Pigman*. HarperTeen.

Other Books by S. E. Hinton

* *Rumble Fish*. Delacorte Press.

Taming the Star Runner. Delacorte Press.

Tex. Delacorte Press.

* *That was Then, This is Now*. Puffin Books.

* NOVEL-TIES Study Guides are available for these titles.

ANSWER KEY

Chapter 1
Vocabulary: 1. a 2. b - S 3. b 4. a - S 5. a - S 6. b 7. a - S 8. b 9. a 10. b - S
Questions: 1. Greasers and Socs were both exclusive gangs: all-male, violent, territorial, bigoted, and threatened by each other. The Greasers were poor. They had black leather jackets, jeans, and greased hair. They were resentful of money and its power. The Socs were affluent. They were well-dressed, well-groomed, and disdainful of poor kids. 2. On the way home from the movies, Ponyboy was beaten by the Socs. He was alone and the Socs saw the opportunity to fight a Greaser. 3. The other Greasers chased the Socs and were concerned about Ponyboy's well-being. His brother Darry was angry that Ponyboy had been foolish enough to walk alone. 4. Darry got upset with Ponyboy because he really loved him and had all the responsibility for Ponyboy and the family. Ponyboy believed that Darry didn't like him very much. 5. Ponyboy and his brothers were different from other hoods and greasers because they hadn't gotten into serious trouble with the police; Sodapop had a job; Ponyboy was a good student; Darry won an athletic scholarship to college, but couldn't use it because he had to work.

Chapter 2
Vocabulary: 1. nonchalant 2. fiery 3. roguish 4. law-abiding 5. scatterbrained 6. bicker
Questions: 1. The Greasers gathered at Ponyboy's house, wandered the streets, hung out at shopping centers, and socialized with other Greasers. 2. Dally ignored the law as a form of defiance against society. 3. It was surprising that Cherry was attracted to Dally because she was a respectable girl from the right side of town; she admired Dally because he was tough. 4. In a "fair" gang fight there were no weapons, just fists; it involved the same number of people on each side. 5. The Greasers resented the Socs' wealth, the accompanying advantages, and their snobbish attitudes.

Chapter 3
Vocabulary: 1. a 2. c 3. d 4. a 5. b
Questions: 1. Cherry thought the Greasers showed their emotions while the Socs did not. Ponyboy felt that both gangs had problems and were not happy. 2. The Greasers' lives were a constant struggle because they had no money and had difficult domestic problems. 3. Ponyboy had slept for so long that the stars appeared to be in different positions. 4. When Ponyboy finally came home, Darry was very angry and slapped Ponyboy. Darry behaved this way because he was very worried about Ponyboy. 5. To change his life, Ponyboy decided to run away. He changed his mind when he started thinking about his home, his bed, and Sodapop.

Chapter 4
Vocabulary: 1. c 2. d 3. f 4. g 5. b 6. e 7. a 8. h; 1. reformatory 2. bootlegging 3. groggy 4. unceasingly 5. apprehension 6. territory 7. contemptuously 8. self-preservation
Questions: 1. The Socs came looking for Ponyboy and Johnny because they had been seen with Socs' girls. 2. Johnny was not a violent person but he was frightened that Ponyboy would be hurt by the Socs. 3. Ponyboy and Johnny turned to Dally for help because they knew he would understand their predicament. Dally gave them money and a gun and told them to hide in an old abandoned church in another town. 4. Ponyboy believed that he and Johnny would be fugitives forever because they were in too much trouble to return home. Johnny would face capital punishment and Ponyboy would be sent to a reformatory.

Chapter 5
Vocabulary: 1. c 2. d 3. e 4. a 5. b; 1. imploring 2. eluded 3. reluctantly 4. vital 5. sullen
Idioms: 1. I couldn't believe what I saw, so I looked again. 2. We made the time pass more quickly. 3. I wanted a cold drink very badly. 4. You look like you've had a rough time. 5. We became sick to our stomachs.
Questions: 1. When Ponyboy awoke in the church, he felt homesick and frightened about what had happened. 2. It became clear that Johnny cared for Ponyboy when he got the supplies, his favorite book, bought bleach, and cut Ponyboy's hair to change his appearance. Also, he allowed Ponyboy to sleep on his shoulder. 3. The boys needed to change their appearances so they would not be caught. Since hair was so important to a Greaser, it was not easy for them to change their hair color and style. 4. To pass the time in the church, the boys played poker and read *Gone With the Wind*. 5. Johnny loved Dally because he would always be cool and calm, almost gallant, in a rough situation. 6. Dally told the boys that Darry was very upset that they left home, that Cherry had become a spy for the Greasers, and that there was going to be a big fight between the Greasers and the Socs.

Chapter 6

Vocabulary: 1. b 2. a 3. d 4. c 5. b

Questions: 1. Cherry decided to help the Greasers because she didn't think they were responsible for Bob's death. 2. Johnny decided to give himself up because he thought this would help him get off easier since Bob's death was really an accident. 3. Ponyboy and Johnny went into the burning church because there were children inside. 4. The boys were all injured from the fire, especially Johnny. 5. Ponyboy realized that Darry loved him when Darry hugged him and was holding back tears. 6. Ponyboy felt that he had come home for good because now he knew that Darry really cared for him.

Chapter 7

Vocabulary: 1. f 2. e 3. g 4. b 5. d 6. a 7. c; 1. palomino 2. mimic 3. individual 4. aghast 5. manslaughter 6. recurring 7. genuine

Questions: 1. Television reporters were interested in the boys because they were already infamous for murdering Bob. Now they were heroes for saving the children in the burning church. 2. As a result of the fire, Johnny was badly burned and had a broken back. Ponyboy worried that Johnny would be crippled for the rest of his life. 3. From the newspaper, Ponyboy learned that he might be separated from his two brothers and sent to a home because of the recent trouble. 4. Randy wanted to tell Ponyboy that he wasn't going to fight in the rumble. 5. Randy was tired of fighting because he felt there could be no winners. Fighting would not change anything. 6. The boys concluded that gangs could be made up of individuals who thought and acted independently. Belonging to a gang did not mean acting and thinking in concert.

Chapter 8

Vocabulary: 1. c 2. d 3. e 4. a 5. f 6. b; 1. faltered 2. resemblance 3. charitable 4. debate 5. quivering 6. numb

Questions: 1. Johnny was nearing death because the doctor did not think it could hurt him to have company. 2. Ponyboy meant that you only see the negative side of life on the streets—poverty, fighting, angry people. 3. Johnny did not want to see his mother because she had always misunderstood and rejected him. 4. Dally was going to use the knife to force his way out of the hospital to attend the rumble. 5. Ponyboy was upset with Cherry because she refused to see Johnny in the hospital, blaming him for killing Bob.

Chapter 9

Vocabulary: 1. miniature – small in scale 2. grimaced – made a contorted facial expression 3. mock – fake 4. amplifier – electronic device to increase sound 5. escort – person accompanying another

Questions: 1. Before the fight, Ponyboy took a shower and changed his clothes. He did this to bolster his confidence and to show that he was just as good as the Socs. He put oil in his hair to show he was proud of being a Greaser. 2. Darry thought Ponyboy was in bad physical condition and might, therefore, put himself at risk in the fight. 3. Dally told Ponyboy that if you are tough you won't get hurt as Johnny did. Answers to the second part of the question will vary. 4. Johnny meant that Ponyboy should not get old and cynical, but stay young and hopeful about the future.

Chapter 10

Vocabulary: Across—3. impact 6. dumbfounded 9. editorial 10. triumph; Down—1. bruise 2. concussion 4. indignant 5. vacant 7. daze 8. delirious

Questions: 1. Ponyboy kept repeating that Johnny wasn't dead because he couldn't accept the truth. 2. Dally was shot and killed. Answers to the last part of the question will vary, but may include the idea that he did plan his own death because he was angry and hurt when Johnny died. 3. Ponyboy believed that other Greasers would end up like Dally because they would not stop fighting or getting into trouble. It seemed inevitable that they would come to a bad end. 4. Ponyboy was hospitalized due to a concussion he received during the rumble and as a result of general exhaustion. He collapsed as the police came to pick him up with other Greasers. 5. When Ponyboy regained consciousness, he thought about his friends who died, about his future which would be decided by the courts, and about his relationship with Darry.

Chapters 11, 12

Vocabulary: 1. e 2. b 3. f 4. c 5. d 6. a; 1. familiar 2. calm 3. vague 4. cautious 5. vast 6. convicted

Questions: 1. When Ponyboy looked at Bob's picture, he realized that Bob was a real person who had been very important to Cherry and Randy. 2. Randy visited Ponyboy because he still felt guilty about what happened, and he was concerned that he had disappointed his father. 3. At the hearing, Ponyboy feared the judge would separate the brothers. 4. Due to his concussion and his emotional turmoil, Ponyboy still thought he was responsible for Bob's death. 5. Ponyboy was surprised by the judge's questions because he thought the judge would ask him more questions about Bob's murder. 6. The judge dismissed the case; therefore, the brothers would not be parted. Answers to the second part of the question will vary. 7. Darry scolded Ponyboy so that he would snap out of his trance, work hard, and make something of himself. Sodapop couldn't bear to see his two brothers fighting so much, and he was upset over the loss of his girlfriend. 8. In his message to Ponyboy, Johnny wanted to be sure Ponyboy would always appreciate the beautiful things in life, such as a sunset. Answers to the second part of the question will vary. 9. The contents of this novel, *The Outsiders*, was Ponyboy's English theme. He wanted to use this experience to explain that the Greasers were real people with unique personalities like everyone else. Perhaps his words would communicate hope to other young people who considered themselves "outsiders."

NOTES: